TEDDY BEAR, TEDDY BEAR,
SCHOOL DAY MATH

Barbara Barbieri McGrath
Illustrated by Tim Nihoff

SCHOLASTIC INC.

Teddy Bear, Teddy Bear,
school's begun.
Count the teddies.
Join the fun!

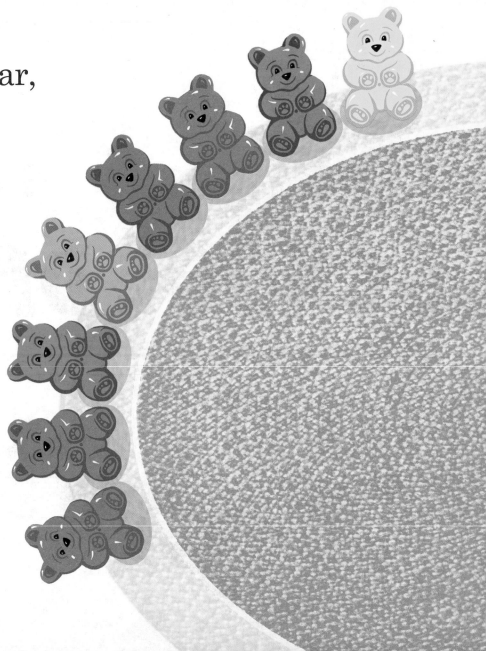

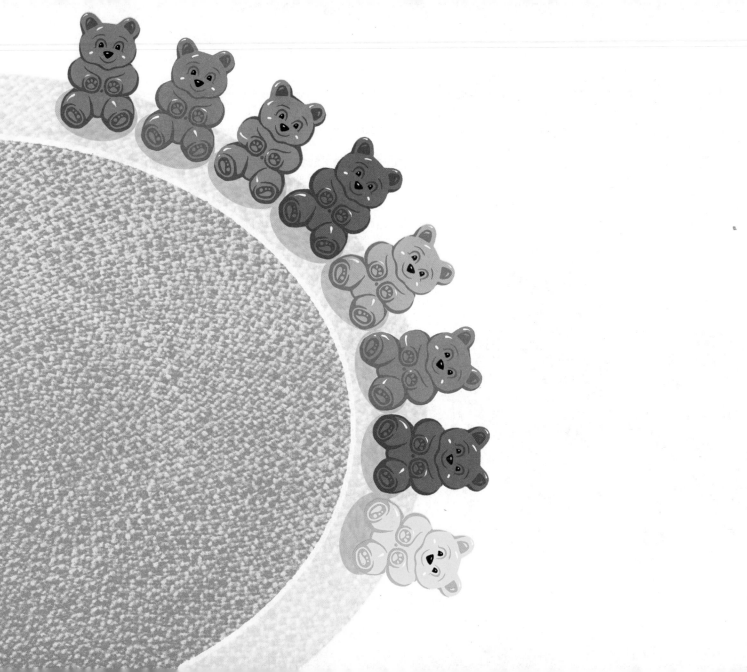

Teddy Bear, Teddy Bear,
sit up straight.

Count by twos.
Do you see eight?

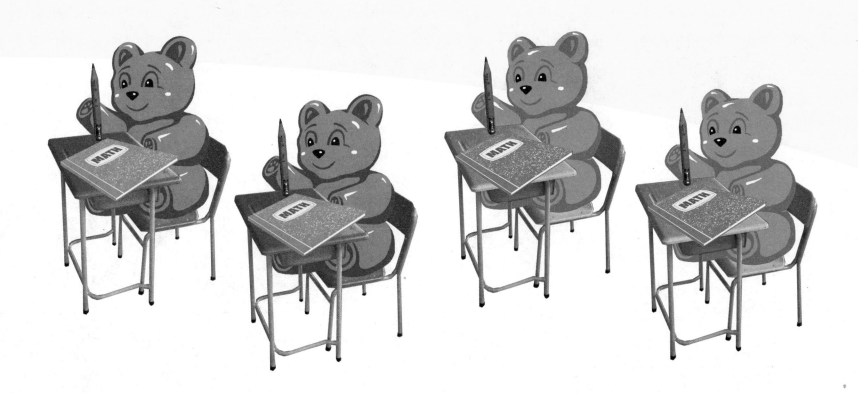

Teddy Bear, Teddy Bear,
touch the floor.

Which group of bears
has just four?

Teddy Bear, Teddy Bear,
pat your head.

Are there fewer
yellow or red?

Teddy Bear, Teddy Bear,
turn around.

Which weighs more?
Good! Sit down!

Teddy Bear, Teddy Bear,
say your age.

How many bears
are on this page?

Teddy Bear, Teddy Bear,
blow, blow, blow!

Which teddy comes next
in this row?

Teddy Bear, Teddy Bear,
time to drive.
Which of these groups
has more than five?

Teddy Bear, Teddy Bear,
fly, fly, flew.

How many is one bear
plus these two?

Teddy Bear, Teddy Bear,
tie your shoe.

Are there fewer
green bears or blue?

Teddy Bear, Teddy Bear,
moo like a cow.

Which color bear
should line up now?

Teddy Bear, Teddy Bear,
clap and shout.

How many are left
when three sneak out?

Teddy Bear, Teddy Bear,
save a penny.
Count by fives
to see how many.

Teddy Bear, Teddy Bear,
a great big laugh.

Which teddy bear
is a bear in half?

Teddy Bear, Teddy Bear,
jump or hop.
Teddy Bear, Teddy Bear,
this means STOP!

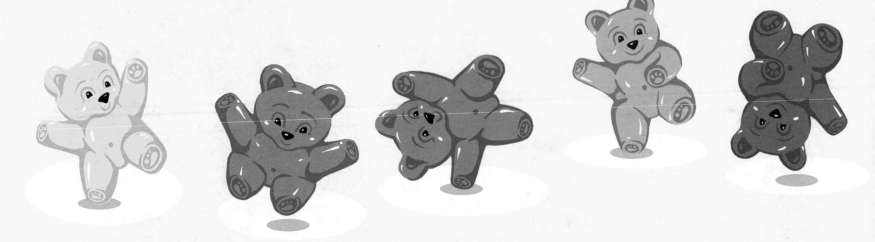

ISBN 978-0-545-59731-9

Text copyright © 2012 by Barbara Barbieri McGrath.
Illustrations copyright © 2012 by Tim Nihoff. All rights reserved.
Published by Scholastic Inc., 557 Broadway, New York, NY 10012,
by arrangement with Charlesbridge Publishing. SCHOLASTIC and
associated logos are trademarks and/or registered trademarks of
Scholastic Inc.

12 11 10 9 8 7 6 5 4 3 2   13 14 15 16 17 18/0

Printed in the U.S.A.   40

First Scholastic printing, September 2013

Illustrations hand drawn digitally and collaged with
found objects in Adobe Photoshop
Display type set in Animated Gothic and text type set
in Century Schoolbook
Designed by Whitney Leader-Picone

A bear hug to Branson.—B. B. M.

Debby Dargan (Art) + Ed Teska (Math) = Love
I cherish your sweet, playful, and mindful
teachings.—T. N.